Angry Yello

Vera Chok

Burning Eye

BurningEyeBooks
Never Knowingly
Mainstream

This edition published by Burning Eye Books 2024

www.burningeye.co.uk

@burningeyebooks

Burning Eye Books
15 West Hill, Portishead, BS20 6LG

ISBN 978-1-913958-47-3

Angry Yellow Woman is the debut poetry collection from Vera Chok. Is Vera a woman, though? And how yellow are they? The anger is real. These playful, searching, and violently sexy pieces expose Vera's immigrant-hobo journey through the landscapes, beds, and bodies of the UK and beyond. They're a record of how—and where—Vera has tried to locate safety and joy. At the ends of the earth, or down Bethnal Green station? This colonised body seems stuck—flat nose pressed up against the window of Tesco, Chinese eyes wide, hungry. Mouth sighing Malay.

'Visceral, gut-punching, compelling. Vera Chok is one to watch.'
HELENA LEE

'Searing, soaring words. This is a glorious, furious exhalation.'
MUSA OKWONGA

'Vera Chok is a writer, actor, connector, and warrior, picking at the edges of representation, writing nakedly about the complexities of race and desire.'
CRESSIDA KOCIENSKI

'Like nothing I've come across before. The way Vera uses words as an experimental medium to rhyme ideas and sound and language is so exciting, new, contemporary and emotive.'
ELLA FRADGELEY

The phrase *yellow peril* (sometimes *yellow terror* or *yellow spectre*), coined by Kaiser Wilhelm II of Germany, in the 1880s, after a dream in which he saw the Buddha riding a dragon threatening to invade Europe, blends Western anxieties about sex, racist fears of the alien other and the Spenglerian belief that the West will become outnumbered and enslaved by the East.

Leung Wing-Fai, *Perceptions of the East*

Foreword

As you read these poems out loud, or in silence, or with the relevant musical cues playing, you might decide, as Vera once instructed an editor, to 'treat it like concrete poetry'. Or you could approach it as though listening in to conversations, walking through a crowded place getting poked at by memory, as an investigation into the plasticity of language – or, to quote the poet again, as a 'scream at cultural and spatial constrictions'. The settings change, continents are traversed, and characters, both animal and human, delight in language to sublime and sometimes violent absurdity.

What marks them all out as uniquely *Chokian* is the individuality of each poem's situation, intention and melody whilst retaining an anarchic freedom of expression which, to quote Vera, feels 'like I'm allowed to exhale and laugh and unfold. POP!'

Many of the poems in this collection have percolated for over a decade. They have been read aloud by different voices, recorded, performed live, marked, and judged as award-winning anti-slam material. These poems have lived in performance for many years already; have exhaled and laughed and unfolded between poet and audience. This is what gives them such a striking muscularity on the page; the physicality of the poet when performing is inherent in and inseparable from the rhythm of these pieces.

I first read what would become 'Maps, or X Marks the Spot' on 6 October 2013. Along with the text of the poem Vera included this note:

> I started off intending to write something that could be performed but also experienced on the page. I ended up with something which was more for the page … Semi-autobiographical and including edited parts of poems I'd written this year, this ended up as a study on place and truth, real and imagined. I am interested in:
>
> • (subjective) points of view and the evocative and manipulative nature of language e.g. place names.
> • fiction vs fact, subjective memory and multiple narratives

- *conjuring and confusing sensory experiences*

It might end up as part of a compilation of thoughts on place, personhood, finding, losing and creating.

On first reading I thought the piece was 'a beautiful thing. I would happily have this as a hardback piece of art to drink in at will, it is so FULL of shape and of space and of searching and stopping.' The fact that this piece now exists as part of *Angry Yellow Woman* feels right; the fact that Vera offers it up as a performance piece for us to inhabit ourselves reveals the generous curiosity of the anthropologist within.

Of *scritch*, the 2017 collaboration between Vera, myself and Serena Braida, a friend commented that 'as a reader you feel like one of the gang; a silent collaborator'. This is how I have felt when reading certain poems included here. 'A Knife in the Dark' is an invitation to a silent collaboration, while 'Mysterious Girl' taps into the confronting truth of that same invitation.

Vera recently described the publication of this collection as 'like me shedding skin or something'. It is a playful, confronting, musical, searching, and anarchically intimate skin. This intimate anarchy comes from the fact that Vera 'can't leave the room when I'm feeling uncomfortable, only the paying audience and the people in power can do that. I have to be present, in the moment, all of my skin and all of my feelings do.'

In fact, the more I try to write about Vera's poems, the more her own words seem to be the only satisfying introduction, and so, rather than delay your introduction to the poetic 'POP!' of Chok, I'll follow some sound advice and leave the poems to grow how and where they will. As Vera has said, 'I think of seeds and the wind. We just have to let them land where they do, and how they grow, or if they grow, is beyond us.'

Gloria Sanders
London, 2024

CONTENTS

PROLOGUE

The Presentation and (Re)presentation of the Foreign Body, or The Performativity of Self for the Oriental Woman #Intersectionality, or My White Boyfriend Is Better Than Yours

A piece for two 100% authentic Chinese poetesses. A response to the outrage of British boy poets when Sarah Howe – too young, beautiful and Chinese – won the TS Eliot Prize in 2016. First performed at the Oxford Anti-Slam 2016, a tournament where the 'worst' poem wins.

Bowie's 'China Girl' plays. Two cheongsam-wearing, female-presenting, Chinese-looking bodies totter onto stage. They are more than presentable. We watch them wriggle and whisper to the white judges on stage. All girlish wiles. Poetess 1 speaks with a heavy Chinese-y accent, while Poetess 2's accent is RP. Microphones are used to amplify the seduction.

Poetess 1:
My white boyfriend is better than yours
He has no armpit hair
He shaves it off because
I liiiiiike it!
He shaves behind closed doors
The hair on his broad white back is
very, very sexy
I like to stroke it when I'm stressed because
you know, London is very stressful
You stroke things you can get
you know, like cats
When I'm seeking inner peace
When I'm seeking inner peace

Poetess 2:
Yeah, we're from London
but I used to study here so
I have a connection with Oxford

My white boyfriend is better than yours
He sings such nice Chinese
All seven tones of Cantonese
And he's a scholar of the mutually
unintelligible dialects Mandarin,
Hokkien, Teochew, Hainanese,
Hakka

Wow
Mm
(murmurs something Chinese)

They tend to begin with the letter H
I don't know why that is because
I don't speak Chinese at all

My white boyfriend is better than yours
His thighs are like a horse, neigh!
Stampedes! And cracks!
my gilded shrine
Make way for his biiiiig
wurst   (Penis)

My white boyfriend is better than yours
Cuts through clouds of cloudy incense with heady
sweat and musk
My white boyfriend shatters the smooth glass of
my inscrutable Chinese face

(something else in Chinese)

In unison:
My white boyfriend conquers my furrows
Irrigates
good earth

Poetess 1:
Draws aside the silk veil…

*The poetesses are struck by the possibility of a world beyond their
white boyfriends.*

Poetess 2:
Takes the fan…
from my hand…

*Bereft, their empty hands reach for each other… their small eyes meet.
Lips part, a gasp! They kiss their lipstick off! Entwined, enmeshed, a
fantasy. Thighs flash, silk stroked. They do not come up for air.*

CHINESE KISSES (THAT'S RIGHT, YOU HEARD ME)

Mysterious Girl

O!
What's in a woman?
That which we call a woman
by any other name would taste as sweet
So woman would, were womb not woman called

They call her mellow yellow
That's right
A mysterious girl
for the night
O, little China girl
Like a bull in a shop I
wreck my
beat my
crash my
China doll
Tragic like thunder
Sh-sh-shhh
Sh-sh-shhh

Boundaries, or I Just Want to be Creative

Stop with the frown, girl, and
lighten up
brighten up
whiten up

Mouths

Is it possible to feel or scratch or long   for
        under
        water
        under
        scales
        without hands   fingercurling fancy
A grain of taste or pain   just the tip
Against rules   dip it in
Break mine   break the rules

Is it possible to hold
        breath thoughts light
Revolve round suns with no shadow   doubt
Noon and soft focus spooning   that's love?
Long conversations
Mouths   (h)ope

Will we drown in
        bed bath bad head
        real estate telly football food
        vino vodka money ghouls
        children travails you

In out
Lights off
In out
Ah

Bees

And the sun brings out all the flowers and the girls
And the bees just wanna get
in
                              thud

A mouse is in the house

I think I need to be frightened
To play some game with some god
To tease some line in some sand to
seeeeeee and feeeeeeel re-ali-ty
FFS!
O! That's what I need
Something slippy

A little mouse in the house
A finger at the door

Nina

Sweat diamonds
Microbe celebrations
Stellar stellar star

As
toes long for
feet I
shun outside to taste the
glow of
birds and breasts and weight

Bumps of skin
Lamplight eyes
A forest lake at night

I would cast my sword for thee
Hum words to reach some deep
Would mine rough seas
And hide us
A harbour of sweet sheets
in breakfast-crumbed delight

Commonwealth

A man from Australiah
Brown skin, large hands
broad soft tongue
Spectacled
Wounded
A face that said yes
A military man with a wide
white smile
Young at the time and
smooth
Strong from mixed bloods and
simplicity

But still I bled
Washed my feet of sand
and
let him
Not pain but
Nice to leave sometimes
Body past edges

Where can we go to shout (do we ever get to shout)
Where is that finger, two or three or four, and
how do we ever meet again on
foreign foreign land
both out at sea

A brown-skinned white man and me

Australiah
Who got where (there)
Who came
first

Haibun

Sunday morning at Tesco Metro, in busy Bethnal Green. A bright green beacon backpack on and very flat shoes. I pass the hip-height trolley and my telephone rings. I set down metal basket and speak. To my father. The doors slide open shut again on occasional repeat. He is on the equator hot. He hears my tears.

> Air escapes sometimes
> Overstretched in no map land
> Alive parched alive

Saturday evening unusual activity. Past the glass and metal jewellery store in the air-controlled mall. Canary Wharf a cave above. 'This is where I bought a shiny wedding ring.' I stop. In silent, slow, motion, a teen love letter unspools. February 15th, many years ago. He wrote in black and blue, then, and now, still, a fist: 'You haven't changed a jot.'

> Sovereign princess
> Do not love him your way
> The power you give is loss

Any late night. The blue or green or brown of eyes, skin, fawn hair, and mouth. Cotton sheets, fairy lights, and foxes sleeping tight. A still-life flick. But then desire: a hammer. Smash their atoms in, drop them on my tongue, my skin. O, to sew new buttons on their coat, cook stew, and burn stars out with!

> Open-mouthed moon
> One world points to another
> No skin between our cells

The only nice one

O John!
The first nice one
Hometown Stirling noticed me
red hair, tongue pierced, and out of place
Your lovely
chink for squeezes
You kept me safe from shame, though
Far, far from home

O John!
My first nice one
The fucks we knew were grrreat
Crumbling stonewall sex and
rosy cold hand   cheeks!
Easy breezy days
Gear from mates and night-time trips
Scotland never felt so good
Lazy laughter days

O John!
The first – nice – one
Adam was your name
And I had got it wrong
A fool, I left to run through fields and fell
and fell again
Lost and crying, tumbling back
You nursed my prickled hands and held me as I
pulled them back to
run and run again

Monster

Ah, I think
Hayfever
That's why I feel so
shit but my pills are
too
far
away
And the tall loud Theys ask
When is Gracie free to
do this and this and this
We love and miss That Girl
And would she like to
make *us* better
And could she just return our calls and
come for walks and tea
And Grace, you must just get on up and out for
More Fresh Air

We love you and *We*
miss you and
Well, whaddaya think she wants?
Under under bed

Stop the monstrous kindnesses
Big solid safety love would make
cups and cups of tea
with
perfect perfect
silent eyes and
quiet silent
teeth

Hardass Street, the friendliest gym in town

Jonny said to Gracie, *Forgive yourself let go live well and what is
more important than your peace and happiness and*
Gracie kept stretching out her hamstrings on the sweaty mat
Leather smacking sounds and that guy who keeps singing and
'90s R&B hits on the stereo-o-o
And an endless stream of tears for who exactly?
10am on a Friday in a boxing gym on Hardass Street, no shit
Car body work going on outside, the last time she walked past a
man was on his back, howling, *I can't feel it, Mikey, I can't feel my
arm*, and
Cranes and diggers prepping ground for new flats next door and it
was earlier, then
Do ALL her friends want to get in Gracie's pants? That's some story
Is Gracie to blame for her parents' love crash?
Jonny said to Gracie, *Think about it it's not real and*
She looked up at his big black body and thought about her
own
kept stretching
streaming
A puddle of lost salt
Kayla said to Gracie, *Be your own kind of awesome*
Oprah said to Gracie, *Let's meditate!*
Who said, *A cloud doesn't worry about being a cloud and it is part of
everything and it does things when it's the right time and*
Gracie yellow Gracie
kept stretching
kept fearing the man on the street in Brixton on his back, howling
the woman who didn't say hi at yoga
the lorry driver in Penang who sped round corners and blared his
horn at short skirts
the dark-skinned coolie

Jonny said to Gracie, *We're not allowed to have tea in the café any
more, management doesn't*

like it, doesn't like
– people talking –
IT
And as soon as Gracie
left, she couldn't
recall a thing

What's more important
more important than tomatoes turning red
more important than what that Jonboy said

Ici, ici, Mrs Wholebelly

Inspired by Sophie Herxheimer's kitchen

I
Accelerate to
    The Department of Surprising Pan Amplification
    The Royal Nation of Portions
    The Regiment of the Science of Nourishment
    The Ministry of Rich Colour Livings and All the Trimmings

II
Tilt by, lilt by, stop
You caught me by surprise, Mrs
A slippy toothy stop
Smash *everything*, Mrs Wholebelly? One by one or not?
Plate after plate after plate after plate after cup after cup after cup?
Vase after dish after joy or woe
A spot of tea and gin to go!

You are more than all to me
You laugh onto me and glow
And paint, my god, the marks you make
The words from which you flow

There is something of me in this, I think
There is something of me, I know

    Home and hearth and food and feelings
    Dogs and books and warmth and reading
    And miles to go before I sleep, and miles to go before I sleep

Smash everything, Mrs Wholebelly
Smash every single thing
For a Rose-headed Future
For a Rose-headed Future

III
Winsor Emerald, Rouge Vif, Havannah Lake, Geranium
Bengal Rose, Rose Tyrien, Rose Malmaison
Mimosa Yellow, Brilliant Yellow
Egg AND chips

Kiss Feet

I got into bed with this boy
and we made lovely long
lines
Wove tales to bind us
Licked lips to wind us deeper into
night
Touched through sheets

    Face east for love, my love
    Share with me sweet sleep
    Kiss feet and toes, my love
    Tomorrow almost mine

Will you
bee my bee, bee,
before summer's
out?

Will you
bee my bee, bee,
before summer's
out?

After Joan Didion, or An Anthropology

It is now, as I begin to write this, the evening of May 12, 2017.

Five months and seventeen days ago, at approximately five o'clock on the morning of November 25, 2016, my friend and guardian angel, Noel Christopher Giff, appeared to (or did) experience, in the cold hospital bed where over a day ago I had left him sleeping, an X that caused his death. I had said to him, left him a note, even, 'See you tomorrow, Chris! Love you!' On the 24th, I was on the sofa at a friend's, watching a doc. Shark's Fin, the unclimbable 4,000-foot peak of Mount Meru. A mountaineering doc. The Himalayas. I watched the men risk their lives, break bones, lose loved ones. Their wives stayed at home.

Twitter, what should I do about my dying friend? Take time off, they said. Self-care, and protect. Celebrate the birth of a friend and Thanksgiving too. Practice practice kind self-care. Take a break from death.

Chris never left St Bart's. Not for weeks, or months. He wanted to die at home. His family didn't know. The doctors didn't listen. Not to him, not to me. The doctors were too tired. So was I, so was he. Chris just wanted to pee, to stop paying bills. His family, his family, his family didn't know.

Two women stood around while Chris held his cock. Tomorrow, Chris, we would die a little, so let's lie back and try a little. He wanted dancing at his funeral. His family didn't know.

This is my attempt to make sense of the period Now that might cut loose ideas I have about love, life, probability and luck, angels and spirits, money and marriage, devotion and class. Legacy. About the ways in which we do and do not follow blood and joy, about the shallowness of sanity, culture, about Y, Y, itself.

I have been a meaning-maker since year Z. A writer since nought. Meaning resides nowhere. We want to die at home.

NATIVE SPEAKER CREDIBILITY

NATIVE SPEAKER CREDIBILITY IS
A POTATO IN SPACE
AND BALLYTURK'S

                              The panic tree's on Jelf!

THE DISTANCE BETWEEN LOVERS
SEVEN LIGHT YEARS AWAY
IS GONE, GONE FOREVER, BUT O! MY WHITE
BOYFRIEND
IS BETTER THAN YOURS

In the beginning there was
there is
a starting girl point

ONE

No one is ready. Someone speaks:
    A shared universal humanity
Spotlight. The action of building. An unstable vertical structure.
Build, clamber, clammy, speak.
    That human beings are –
    at this moment, in history, into the future – fundamentally
    made of stuff that separates us from animals?
    Motherlove, morality, kinship, caring
    Creatures ranging over a spinning sphere
    suspended in space
    Yesterday, today, into perpetuity
    PerPETuity

    If we could reproduce like paramecia do you think that we
    would not, pet?
    Hey, perp! If we could reproduce like bananas do you
    think that we would not?

> *The banana (Musa acuminata) is a berry formed from a superior ovary*
> *of three joined carpels arranged in an axile placentation. The flowers*
> *are born and borne on long and pendulous inflorescence that are*
> *usually unisexual, that is, the female flowers are bored near to the*
> *base of the peduncle (producing the typical banana berry fruits) whilst*
> *the male flowers board on the tip of the same peduncle. Seed may*
> *be produced or, more usually, develop the berry parthenocarpically.*
> *Both the seeded and the parthenocarpic berry are very similar in*
> *structure when flowering.*

Placentation pendulous peduncle producing
pathenocarpically parthenocarpic berry
Placard postman poostick puncture patchwork peabrain pleb

Wait. Bananas are berries?

(unreadable) 1908
SS Delfina, Sydney, Australia

Dear Kate
Just a line to let you know what part of the world I am in. I
have been out hear 6 weeks now and expect to be home for
Xmas. Am going round the coast of Australia and New
Zealand. Give Best Love to G & W and Fred if you can see
him.
I remain Your loving Sweetheart Harold
xxxxxxxxx
xxxxxx

PS Don't forget the message on the Front I keep to it

Noisy, blue electronica. Flashes of reproductive light. Potato faces in the dark.

A VOICE ON A MICROPHONE:
I'll be whatever you want me to be

        wherever
You'll be wherever you want in me   whenever
You'll come over me in any weather

        A dirty trumpet howls
        A-wop-bop-a-loo-bop a-
        wop-bam-boom!

And they-I-we
will do anything for some
affection

SYLVIA: I… don't know why I'm *single*—
TED: I mean it's kind of *weird* to talk about fault *anyway*, like, like there's some kind of *moral obligation to be* with somebody—
SYLVIA: I did something really *silly* yesterday—
TED: Because I'm a bit fed up of, you know, people saying, 'Oh! You're, you're *single!* Why?' Like, er, like, what they *want* to say is, 'What's *wrong?'*
SYLVIA: I contacted somebody, a *boy*, who I thought, he's *really* good looking, and he's sort of, he, h— I don't know! I don't know if I contacted him *because* I wanted to have a fling, because if I *really* think about it I don't think he *reads*—
TED: I mean if you're in *London*, I mean, it's *very* easy to forget you're single—
SYLVIA: I don't think I could date someone who never read *anything*—
TED: You, you can run *all* over the place meeting different people, I mean, so many people *live* here, er, and there's so many *opportunities* to, to get to *know* people, and they're all just an *underground* ride away—

@herxideas Dear Neighbour, I have left the house. My insides roil past the friendly butcher, the workmen, the panic tree on Jelf.

Jones, The Butcher | Meat. The way is meant to be
There has been a flourishing butcher's shop on this site since 1910.
Learn the art of butchery. Our butchers will explain the reasons and science for each cut.

Central line. The red one.

Melt at 300 degrees
50,000 leagues, the faces on that poster, out of date, smiling

I'm attached to my bag, MATE
WHEN YOU PUSH my bag
WHEN YOU PUSH my bag with your bag WHEN YOU PUSH
ANY
PART of your
BODY AGAINST MY BODY YOU PUSH
ME   in front of the train
ASSHOLE

Your body   my death. Limbs lost. Ghosts

My sorryhag, tiredass, longing
                              in front of the train

Drag bad lips across a
face. Droop mouthends
Seal bodies kiss, sweat drying, skin drag

If I asked
you'd lick my ass
So Hum
                              Jump

SYLVIA: So *therefore*, there's no *future* in the relationship. He's not someone I could *really*, at this stage, say I could have a long-term *relationship* with, but I contacted him *anyway*. I said, *'Hey!* How're you doing?' Sort of, *you know*, trying to *maybe* see if he'd like to go out for a drink, but *surely* that's *silly?*

When I kiss my new internet lover –

When I kiss my new internet lover
desravenous
the beats keep my fingers to the keyboards to the hot of your face and
I travel
slugsaliva
saltbutter Marmite
bisongrass cut
plain ready
feet contracted but

SYLVIA: I couldn't *marry* someone who didn't read books—

please
Please
pulse
pulverise
Pessimist!
pinktron
panther
juice

Heyyy

bee!
What's your little bee-cunt like?

Flower-fragrant, pollen-filthy, buzzed up
bee

Hey, bee!
Stick it where it hurts and –
Stripey-jumpered, furry-assed, and Ripped
Right
Out – **O, Bee!**
Self-murder is sweet and
tinybit proboscis licks
small stamps on Sundays

If I had posted my letter
Sent it north cold
Cold

TED: There are *advantages* to being with somebody on a regular
basis, or even *living* with somebody—
SYLVIA: I don't *know*… it's *difficult* 'cause I, in a way, I *am* quite sexist
and I *do* want to be at home and, I *don't know*, have a *really* fantastic
meal waiting—
TED: I li— I *like* the idea that I can say that this, *this* space is *mine*,
and *that space* is *yours* and *maybe* there's a space in the middle that
is *our* space and we can *both* occupy that space, but there's *always*
room to sort of *escape* and re— what's the word, re—

                                                        like a woman
                                        expectant at some crossing or other
                                    some journey to an idea of an outside world
                                            the sludge of sewers seen and embraced
                                                            a woman
                                                        quite beautiful
                                                he and she and it and they
                                                    At the point of jumping

Nothing Is Really Difficult, or Princess

Tender is
black-haired doll
arranges pans and clatters cutlery

Signorita dreaming

Set the sea to simmer, dance
Swell like hearts swell
There's emerald childhood grass there

Burn tongues, swirl talk and
sing with silk-embroidered bandits, rabbits
Principessa
Seven nights a week
                          none of this is mine
Wind blurs us
Scenery adapts
floating
white
laminate

Principessa prin ci pessa
Principes pes sa
Principessa principessa
principess

Not Lambeth Walk

A flat in Shepherd's Bush. Acton, really
Some body doesn't live here anymore
This songlyric view of the same piano in '84, '95 or '02
This afternoon in this flat
The meadow where they filmed the Flake advert
      I know the feeling
      Steel, glass, and charcoal grey
      A glossy magazine. Media company gittishness
          Cause *beacon* effect
It's a complicated place – the Grand Canyon, children, my bed
Canterbury Cathedral or Stonehenge – the same
A monument, a valley, a semi-detached O
          What?
A small French village at absolute dawn
An impossible romantic memory at dawn
          That is a place
A hole in the ozone layer, the moon, a place called Brimham Rocks
It doesn't matter what time

TED: I sometimes think, *you know*, if I *died* in my sleep or if I *fell over* in the *bathroom* and hit my *head* or something, *you* know, it would be, I don't *know* what it would be… It would be the *smell* reaching the next-door house or *something*… I suppose that's a bit pessimistic or something. My *friends* might try and call—

God Is Able Salon | Hairdresser
75–87 Ridley Road, London E8
It'll Grow Back | Barber Shop
120 S Broadway, Turlock, CA

A black old woman bent over her shopping cart, walking in wetness of greydaytime Brixton. Romantic poverty. I hate her from here. I. Yellow alien in arcadia. Suppository me, if you like. I'll take it mutely, magnificently, with a smallass ass.

What's a middle-class fool? Ask one and he'll write you a memoir, a memo, a prescription, directions to
nowhere.

Who's a working-class poet? Not that guy down the pub, jigging, probiting.

VOICE ON A MICROPHONE: Would you like that gift-wrapped, sir?

Let's navigate

I don't know where you live, exactly
Your caravan, cabin, your cave
Starting point's a slow stroll
Night-time tales, histories, hills
Moonlight and sugared pills but
soon
A pick-up, the drop-off, a taxi in the night
Torn, worn tickets
A too-early flight
A trip to the coast stopped before
(love) started
This is an exercise in burning oil at sea
Matches. Fingers. Face. Ablaze.
A pierced tongue, an abortion

                                              an error

A Knife in the Dark

This is the place.

She had said one step to the right, fifteen paces past the miniature pond and the laughing cow, and nowhere near the trellis with its scented blooms of winter roses. Oho! A reference to Anton Chekhov! She must have really been in love.

A Frenchman once told me that, in Chekhov, no one ever tells the truth; it is all lies, all a painful game.
    'I love to eat at night.' A lie!
    'Here's some cheese for you.' Liar!
    Sonya, a woman in love, fibs about foodstuffs in lieu of love.

There is something intricate and terrible about the way love is constructed. Perhaps it grows like mushrooms – an alien mesh, spreading and rising to worship a pale moon – when conditions are just so.

Tonight, as I tread softly, in search of a truth, I remember the bodies and think of the worms, locked in a silent, earth-turning underground dance. Which is up and where is down? Can we ever know the souls of those who commit these actions? Perhaps the loaf of bread was snatched to save his starving family, but the elderly baker died of fright and now his wife, alone and without love, lights the ovens no more.

I loved, once. A kind of madness, it seemed. Everything I cared for before burnt away. A Herculaneum.

Ashy ghost stains and the memory of outside.

In the cool of the milky night, here, fifteen paces beyond the miniature pond and the laughing cow, and nowhere near the trellis, my pupils dilate, hungry for answers.

I stop by the rockery and lean for a moment. There is no real rush. Full of fear of what's to come yet, in control, I have brought myself to this place. I have accepted that time will pass – time does pass – and the pain of our loss – yes, it is shared – will pass too.

The surface of the miniature pond reassures me in its almost stillness. Little boatmen skid about in their happy world. I perch on the low stile. After a few quiet moments, the crinkling foil on my lap reveals sandwiches, crusts neatly cut. Cheese and pickle and strangely comforting.

I survey the grounds before me. It's ideal. Idyllic. Everything in its place and nothing out of turn. There, the tennis lawn. There, the orchard with fruit safe from insect jaws. The household dreams of half-term by the sea and the dogs doze by the dying fire with wild rabbits running through their minds. No one will see it coming.

This is where I'll break his heart.

SYLVIA: Again, *logically*, *rationally*, that should be *absolutely fine*, everyone's an *adult*, you know, but if you don't *think* about *why* you're doing what you're doing, then *how* are you supposed to have a relationship?

TED: Was I telling you about my too-late-to-do-anything-about-it, no, I was telling Phil... It's kind of *weird* to talk about *fault* anyway like, like there's some kind of *moral* obligation to *be* with somebody and *propagate*—

SYLVIA: I guess the *main* thing is, do – you *really* have to go and live your own life. I feel *very* strongly about people who say, *oh*, I couldn't help it, er, I just *fell* in love or I fell *out* of love et cetera, but I think we miss – we *underestimate* or we don't *think* about the element of *decision-making* and *choice*—

TED: I mean there's *really* this notion that, if, you know, if you *have* a child you're *entitled* to support from the state, erm, things like *that*, why, why, *why* should not you be *entitled* to support from the state if you *don't* have a child, think of the, think of the *money* you're saving—

We are ham like mussels, starfish
Lobsters on concrete farming wind

Fists

You stretch me and I think
stitches
Knees open to the wind and
threadbare
A soft curling at the shoulders
A sweet spotlick
Gum's for saliva
Threadcount
Sheets
Lay smooth tracks to
Mine
Train-tunnel sex

TED: *Out* of mind—

Was it messy, fear-full
corerocking pretty
weepfully tastefully
contagious

Was fear made worse by
kindnesscool
No one ever knows

Heartbursting rubbertearing
activitychore
Blanket to chew on
more

More
mystery
lumps

A change of smell
Sleeplite crying
Friends 4eva
until we're not

A little bit
electrocution
masturbation
A rubber-stamped return

This is no love
This is the easy stuff
Virtual, a hit
A magic dust distraction
A dollar for the ride for legs lost again
This is the easy stuff
Ignorable puff
Proof you're not dead, marked
A disposable dream
A fleshy outcrop
A cluster, a target
New skin to rip
Cryogenic cleansing

I'm not a fan of the Ice Age, flooding, cycles of extinction, comets, constellations, bicycles, gods. Ugly amphibious attractions to light. Grasping fingers, prehensile hearts, an awareness of creeping, swelling, new, pale growth. Easy murders on no man's land a long way away.

Jesus! Fuck me sideways!

You gonna slap me around, tough guy?
Make me see sense in this seesaw world?
You gonna lie on your back
punch out truths and tales?
Tongue guy
Ass man
Small tits and
legs and
right up to
squeezing
Stretch
Punch out boredom
Put in some time
Excavate, hoary fingers
Explain
flight on strings
the kickass car
hunger to sleep in just one second
What's in those pockets, and
do you eat yours?
Suck it
Fists, man
Fists

SYLVIA: So yes, I *don't* think I'm clingy in that way, I think I just need someone to be honest about *who* they are and to see me as I really am because there's nothing *worse* than someone projecting their ideals or insecurities onto someone else as if the other person was a *blanket*, canvas, and *you know*, ERROR could make things *better* just by being a, a, a, a, *human being* in their, *on* their, their HORROR eyes and, um, so but, BUTT ROBOT that's already quite, you'd think it'd be quite *easy* to find other human beings, other *adults* who f-FELLLLLLLT this way but I think it's *rare* as a pear in the square out there don't stare at the mare, alotofpeoplearen'tverybrave or COURAGEOUS, because you need a *lott*ov courage – *To A Bee!* – HONEST.

A flush behind the ear
Cold finger loving
Sew without spectacles
my love for your child

Non-white dads talk to their kids too
Walk with them, like everyone else,
through tunnels underground
Tell them why it is they read the
news and
how that man can't live

We spot her knees
The old, thin woman
always there by noon
Eyeshadow blue, singing her tunes
Her cold, white knees old
They have each other
Beautiful

And dad, son, you, we
We say nothing

TED: Who was it who said that the perfect, the *prefct*, the *pefct partner* is, is all very well but can't make you dinner or something. I can't remember.

58

SYLVIA: And yeah, I *wouldn't* st— I wouldn't *stay* in a dead-end relationship given a *long enough* period of time to realise it was a dead-end relationship, um, because I *do* invest a *lot* in the other person, *actually.* Invest is a *terrible* word, it sounds as if I want stuff *back*—
TED: But once it's too late that's *it*—
SYLVIA: But *surely* you'd stop doing something that distressed the person you were *supposed* to be in love with—

        A long-distance call from a white man in Singapore.

TED: Um—

Five thousand square metres of gleaming Neue Nationalgalerie, eight hundred metres' worth of wall, black anodised aluminium, inside, out. Think with your tongue. Lick, draw. Draw the surface, breathe with your mouth. Before disintegration. Skyscrapers. Scree!

I will smash your watch, Timekeeper. Fling it past the garden fence for foxes, parakeets. Place it on your jogging path with a piss-weak strap. Send it to Coventry, Rotherham. Never tell it how *Wuthering Heights* ends. Won't feed it pikelets in Halifax, nor walk it, slowly with a choc-ice to the end of Southend Pier. The brass bell rings and rings for the bodies at sea, bobbing, bobbing, slow-motion sinking. Suckling oysters chewed alive.

We all have our secondary devices
Things don't die; they fragment

All right, sweetie, come along, come along. I'll pick you up at nine. We'll drive and stroll and snog and sex and make out in your car. Like tadpoles in a jar. Obfuscate with words? No thanks! Wriggle bellies, lick between fingers, I'll pull your hair with feeling.

SYLVIA: A *boy* told me, a boy *relative*, said there's *no reason why* I should be single, *why* – because he says, um, I'm not unattractive and I'm probably *not bad* in bed—

A German sausage dog, excited on a train. A German train. An energy drink in Germany. A German train. Look at the wheels on that!

SYLVIA: I'm *sure* the idea of love, or the *concept* of love, the *feelings* between you, they *must* change but you change *with* the person—
TED: I have a friend who was pregnant recently and, er, *apparently* she snored during her pregnancy, and I *did* share a bed with somebody who snored for about a *month*, no, it *must* have been longer, and, um, it was a *nightmare*—
SYLVIA: And part of, part of being *alive* is having a *forward* momentum but also being *open* to things *happening* to you, um—
TED: Because *obviously* you can roll them over, um, and I don't *remember* who first gave me that piece of advice, but it's *great*, it's *great advice*, it *works*, but, and, you go back to sleep and you sleep for a little bit *but* in the *back of your mind* there's *always* the fear that they're going to *roll* themselves onto their back again and start *all* over again, and it's a bit like de-icing the freezer, you *know*, you *do* it and it's *done*, and *immediately* you close the door and you think, *the ice is coming! The ice is coming!*

This is the pond I fish in
To catch a goldfish and grow a whale and build a home and from its ribs
a white pickle fence of

teeth

Jamaica, 28 July 1970

My love,

*Anerica is fantastic,
but you are not with
me so America is
no good. I am on
my way back to
You darling*

Love W

She holds her tail
for comfort

TED: Do I have to tell that whole story again?

VERA CHOK'S
MEGA DANCE PARTY XXX

Human speech is like a cracked cauldron on which we bang out tunes that make bears dance, when what we want is to move the stars to pity.

Madame Bovary, Gustave Flaubert

Yuddy: I've heard that there's a kind of bird without legs that can only fly and fly, and sleep in the wind when it is tired. The bird only lands once in its life… that's when it dies.
Leung Fung-ying: When did I say I'd come home with you?
Yuddy: You never said you wouldn't.

Days of Being Wild, Wong Kar Wai

Dear Reader,

On my journeys, I have been called many things by many people. Friends, strangers, colleagues, and lovers have all constructed their narratives. My life is either remarkable or unremarkable, depending on one's viewpoint.

I wonder what it takes for human beings to recognise one another. How long can these moments of connection last? We are kept apart by time, geography, education and language. Separated by thin skin, clothing, propriety, speed. And I am always me because I am not you.

But here is something that I made for you. An investigation, a test, a love letter, an aggression, a manifesto, a plea bargain, a way forward or back. I wrote it in a way that might be pleasant for you to read out loud.

Here are some simple instructions for how to navigate your way through:

Who could read this: Anyone, to anyone or to no one.
Where you could read this: Any room, anywhere.
How to read this: You will notice instructions along the way. Interpret them as you like or ignore them altogether.
One rule: Do not voice anything written in grey. Keep this information close, chew it up, spit or swallow.

This book is dedicated to GS and to friends, future and present.

Take Off, or It's Hot in Here

We are in a room. We could be anywhere in the world.
Imagine that you're full of hot, jumping Mexican beans.

Hello, I'm VERA CHOK! and this is VERA CHOK'S MEGA DANCE PARTY XXX!!! WHOOOO!

Pause. How was that? Say it again if you want to.

I like Dancing, Singing, Touching and Tweeting!

Expectant pause.

Here is one of my favourite songs. It makes me very happy.

Find and play 'Me Love' by Sean Kingston (on your phone?)
but the remix version featuring Plies, all klaxons and hard
MCing overlaying this sunshiney tune of love, loss and
nostalgia. It's your favourite song. You cannot help but begin
to dance.

She dances!

VERA CHOK! dances, all limbs and smiles.

This song reminds me of nightclubs in Malaysia! YEEEAAAAH!

VERA CHOK! dances until she sweats.

She dances, she dances!
She dances, she dances, she dances!

You mouth the lyrics. You dance for everyone in the universe; you want them to share your elation.

AAAAHH, I'm HOT!

She dances, she dances!
She dances, she dances, she dances!

Your heart is bursting.

You dance the full three minutes and twenty-five seconds of the song as you read on. You try out new shapes for your body, you see if it's possible to dance to a different rhythm, fighting the beat, you push yourself, you sweat. Your ears go funny, as if you're on a flight, due to the sudden rush of blood to unexpected places.

Oh GOD! I'm tired!

She dances, she dances! She dances, she dances, she dances!

Once,

It's hot!

on a fast train to Paris, Duncan Cameron said, 'VERA CHOK! You're ALWAYS at the wrong parties!'

She dances, she dances! She dances, she dances, she dances!
She dances, she dances! She dances, she dances, she dances!

Once,

Oh God!

on the banks of the Thames, Jonathan Swain said, 'VERA CHOK!
You're ALWAYS heartbroken!'

A thread snags. A slow, private unravelling.

She dances!
She dances!

Arms are too light, legs detach, dancing disintegrates. You
fight for the air you breathe and say:

You know **WHAT**?! I'M SO **HAPPY** TO BE **HERE**!!! **SHE DANCES!**

You're GREAT!!!

She dances, she dances! She dances, she dances, she dances!
She dances, she dances! She dances, she dances, she dances!

The music finally ends. As you collect the pieces, you say,

THIS is great! Hang on,

It's hot!

I have to tweet about this. Get your phone out and send a tweet.

A plane takes off
Swifts curve across the sky
A penguin looks at the moon

If there is such a thing as a
chair in the room it becomes your
platform, your
podium, your
tower, your

An egg fell out of the sky and
met a girl
who lived in a

tree

It said: Gravity doesn't always have to win.

Is anyone else as tired as me?

The panopticon is a structure that was designed by philosopher
Jeremy Bentham as an effective type of surveillance building,
e.g. for a prison. Mind you, the one watching from the tower has
inadvertently allowed themselves to be watched right back.

A bell rings

74

There's No Place Like Home, or Nostalgia is a Disease

With the invention of trains came the invention of shared time.
Our brains didn't explode from the experience of speed and the
universe didn't buckle when we left our homes.

But who else is nostalgic for a forgotten tropical hometown, all
crumbling monuments, fern-invaded shophouses and skinny dirt
roads? Everything's too hot to move, but we'd be easy in our sweat,
flesh and smells. Elderly coconut trees promise the muddy sea
downtown. Remember the pockmarked sand shifting with thousands
of tiny, nervous, translucent-grey crabs? Desultory dogs, stump-tailed
cats, sand flies and cows ignore us. It's foreign and we're free.

I imagine the early morning train that slices a long diagonal across
the peninsula, through rainforests and mountain ranges, reaching
towards the finishing line and rest. An early morning mist lifts over
picturesque old women with leggy village chickens temporarily
hostages in rattan baskets. Brown-skinned children with bright eyes
trot barefoot and wave us off at each station, following the slow train
for half a mile as it too is in the tropics.

It is a place that 'shines into the childhood of all and in which no one
has yet been' – *The Principle of Hope*, Ernst Bloch

A bell rings

Once Broken, Twice Shy

Once upon a time, in a faraway land, there lived a beautiful princess.

Now, it is important to note, at this early stage, that the princess was also intelligent, charming and kind. She had a palatial roof over her head, wasn't short of admirers, and had recently secured a publishing deal with a respectable, if small, house. She was, however, not very well. In fact, she was dying.

What?!

Now, the princess had worked out that she had grown and nurtured so much love in her being that it was poisoning her. An unusual plight, you would be right in thinking.

Now, it's not the done thing to make a fuss over having too large a heart when hurricanes are allowed to rip out planes and flood our lungs, when cyclists are mown down because of the lack of lanes, when trains run off tracks, or when you're suddenly

homeless,

There's a storm outside
It's just glass between me and you
We're all young until the end of time
Nothing's going to fall out of the sky

for instance.

But the princess was going to die, and so she overcame her qualms and sought some counsel.

'Expel it!' yelled the kindly shopkeeper, talking in general terms.

'Use it all up on the next angry, insecure, un-self-aware and emotionally clumsy or alcoholic young man you meet!' screamed her mother.

'My love! Think of yourself as stone, or salt, or fire! Acid, metal or rust! Dig deep or, better yet, fly! In time, everything will be swept away by the cleansing wind. You are the universe and the universe is you!' lowed all the spiritualists and the wise men and women and people of the world.

Everyone was dancing happily, and that's why they were shouting.

Time was running out!

Death is coming!
– Tibetan Buddhist greeting

The princess thought of diving off a cliff and smashing herself up so that something new could grow. (No.)

She exercised. (No.)

She climbed a tree and hung upside down by her hair so that her head would fill with blood so that her heart would shrink.

For a while, the plan worked, but soon enough she swelled into love again, adoring their tiny beaks, their tiny eyes, and their tiny, furious hearts.

It didn't last.

The birds flew away. **They didn't love her back.**

After a good cry, though, it wasn't long till the princess began to imagine the taste and crunch of autumn leaves on her tongue. She swung, long and lazy, within their russet sighs. Eyes closed, she breathed, 'I'll be a tree!' but the leaves left as well, and the princess stayed where she was.

A bell rings

Lightbulbs explode, to capture evidence of a coelacanth swimming,
a ballerina breathing
The light creates temporary constellations in your eyes

A bell rings

Hell Hath No Fury, or The Oriental Woman

You're still up that tree.

In his classic text *Orientalism*, cultural critic and public intellectual Edward W Said proposes that it is distance that creates our desire to know a thing. Asia, or 'The East', in the imaginative landscape, is set apart 'geographically, morally, culturally'.

Dance a little closer, baby.

It's hot!

What d'you want to know? I'm pretty much a straight-A student. I've always been good at both arts and science subjects. I've got a master's degree in archaeology and anthropology from the Queen's College, Oxford, but also passed my preliminaries in Human Sciences, so I know all about genetics, physiology, evolution, statistics, sociology, demography, and anthropology – that's the study of Mankind, you know.

I've fried bacon in greasy spoons and been friends with convicts who've howled my name in the street. I've changed beds and cleaned toilets for a living. I've worked as a vet's assistant, killed puppies, and trained as an auditor. I've shot rifles with Americans and gone sledding with the prime minister of Liechtenstein. I've travelled the world over, one city a week(!), dined in Michelin-starred restaurants and stayed in five-star hotels.

A flutter of wings!

I grew up in Malaysia then moved to England. I lived in London (Herne Hill), Abbots Bromley (Staffs), London (Queen's Park), Abbots Bromley (Staffs), London (Maida Vale), Abbots Bromley (Staffs), London (Isle of Dogs), Oxford (Florey Building), London (Isle of Dogs), Oxford (Back Quad Staircase 4), London (Isle of Dogs), Oxford (Back Quad Staircase 5), London (Isle of bloody Dogs), Oxford (somewhere by the train station), London, Oxford (I nearly bought a house! I married a man! He kissed someone else!), London (Old Kent Road), London (London Bridge), London (Dalston), London (Lower Clapton), London (Bethnal Green), let's tour the country, let's tour the country again, Nottingham, Cumbria, London, London, London. One time, I was sat in bed in a **Travelodge** and ate from a block of cheese. One time, I got to a **Travelodge** and burst into tears – there was no hot water. One time, I reversed the van into a bollard outside a **Travelodge** – I was so tired. One time, near a **Travelodge**, I drove into the back of a car – I was so tired. One time, I drove across the Pennines, past many **Travelodges**, to stare, for an hour, dark-eyed and blind, at the blackening ocean, at a ship of fools.

> Oh, I do like to be beside the seaside!
> Oh, I do like to be beside the sea!
> – a popular British music hall song

In *Journey to the Orient*, the French Romantic poet Gérard de Nerval described the East as 'wonderfully, ingeniously connected to exoticism, glamour and promise'.

'I **promise** you this—'

Churel
Hantu kopek
Langsuir
Penanggalan
Pontianak
Matianak

'—till **death** do us part—'

These are ghosts who fly across the land where I was born, vampires, all of them. They are women who died in childbirth. Their targets are men they might fall in love with, if they were still women.
Men + love = birth = loss

Skimming the skies, their eyes blaze red, their hair's a storm, their insides spill out and trail across the dirt roads, their empty breasts flap, and they wail and shriek and cry, and they wail and shriek and cry, and they wail and shriek and cry in a language you don't listen to.

Pick up. Pick me up.

I see her on the phone
A public payphone at the underground station at those crossroads
we know
Bags at her feet
Open-faced waiting

If I had posted my love letter
Sent it north cold
It would have landed days after hope had died
Days after made-up conversations turned words into sand

I look at the stamp I'd drawn my tongue across

If you had looked
The sun may have warmed your face
But you don't like coconuts

I don't understand your inbetween radio station noise
your open gaping holes of sex fucks dribbling self everywhere
You pretend you can't see, but I sear seek suck
A broken hoover dust-tired
A lassoed twister jerked stuck

You are a small, small soul folded up like a handkerchief
You say
Let's count out some fragile beads to mark our time
What?!
NO! I say
I say
Crush diamonds drawn across thin skin once
Come once and again and whenever you want

Swallow fat food and dance
Eat your sadness and shit it out
Throw off everything – bang goes the chair gone over
Scrawl, crawl, rip open your fingers to write raw open faces
Face me!
More blood! **More** guts!
More than fear is belief, is lov—

Hello? Hello?
Oh, I'm sorry. Belief's not in this morning. Please try again later.

Dial tone.

How do you pick yourself up off the ground when you've never touched down?

Remember you're still up that tree.
Distance is an advantage.

Think of, or point to, someone you might fall in love with and say:

All the better to see you from, my dear. Keep pointing.

In his classic text *Orientalism*, cultural critic and public intellectual Edward W Said credits Gustave Flaubert with creating the enduring picture of the oriental woman as a symbol of 'luxuriant and seemingly unbounded sexuality'.

Strike an excessively alluring pose. Point with your whole being and say:

> I cannot wait until I am there
> I feel the heat on impatient skin
> I bake on a hard deck chair
> My mouth
> parts
> Coming
> up for air
> My arms don't reach far enough fast enough
> Too lazy
> Pinned down by equatorial heat
> Too hot to
>
> Browning like a buttered potato
> sea salted

I know the little beasts that swim and crawl and sing in the swamps rubbing their little legs together

I'm waiting for the crack of my three o'clock thunderstorm

What three things could you say to get a man into bed with you?

I love giving blowjobs. *Strike a pose.* I want you to fuck me in the ass. *Strike a pose.* I am 100% neuroses-free. *Strike a pose.* I'm great in the kitchen. *Strike a pose.*

Wait, that's—

I—

When I was growing up—

My parents met in—

Once, while I was playing with my brother –

I like Dancing, Singing, Touching and Tweeting!

'WHY did you have to GO – O! – away from HOME, love?'

I want a hug **NOW!**

'VERA CHOK! You're ALWAYS at the wrong parties!'

'VERA CHOK! You're ALWAYS heartbroken!'

I climbed a tree and hung upside down by my hair so that my head would fill with blood so that my heart would shrink

I climbed a tree and hung upside down by my hair so that my head would fill with blood so that my heart would shrink

I climbed a tree and hung upside down by my hair so that my head would fill with blood so that my heart would shrink

I climbed a tree and hung upside down by my hair so that my head would fill with blood so that my heart would shrink

I climbed a tree and hung upside down by my hair so that my head would fill with blood so that my heart would shrink

BONG! BONG! BONG!

A thousand million Ice Ages explode at once, the sky opens and meteors stream like party dazzlers, rocks fall on our heads, birds take flight to nowhere, everything is rosy from the blood in our eyes, land disappears and dissolves, and I call out to you, I call out to you,

ADRIAN!!

No response.

ADRIAN!!

No response.

AAAAYYYYY-DREEEEE-UUUUUUUHHHHNNN!!

Listen to this!
I hold my script in my trembling hand: 'I used to think that there was a kind of bird that, once born, would keep flying until death.'

No response.

'The fact is that the bird hasn't gone anywhere. It was DEAD from the beginning!'

No response, no response! No response, no response, no response!

Adrian, it's so POETIC! So TRAGIC! It resonates with ALL my unresolved feelings about **ABCDEFGHIJKLMNOPQRSTUVWXYZEE!**

Adrian, 'Have you heard of a kind of bird—'

Adrian slowly picks up his script and declaims, 'The kind without legs, right? This kind of nonsense can only fool the girls!'

The crowd gasps. The crowd roars. Encore! Encore! An eccentric dance routine. A drum kit rat-a-tat-tats. Wilson, Keppel and Betty clink crystal champagne glasses at the bar. Everything glints and glitters. Blank white sheets fall from the ceiling.

XXX. It's not sex, it's KISSES
A naughty bell rings and rings

Slow

                                   ly
                                Dismount

                              Gymnastics
                is a sport involving Performance
                         Requiring
strength, flexibility, power, agility, coordination, grace and Balance

        There are more women gymnasts than men
      A classic example of a gymnastic dismount is the
we   Flyaway
get

       Elite gymnasts perform difficult variations of
         the flyaway with flips and twists before
down   Landing
       The current system of scoring a routine has
from   dismounts constituting
          a significant portion of a score
       A re-evaluation of this system has been
             called for to encourage
the   Less Difficult Dismounts
         to reduce the number of significant
chair   Injuries

– it used to be a tree –

and

Something in Malay

saya tak boleh tunggu sehingga saya ada
rasa panas pada kulit tak sabar
saya terbakar tas kerusi tu
pokok
pohon
ranting
dedaun
dedaun
dalam mulut
saya
dihanyut udara
tangan tak sampai
cukup jauh cukup pantas
bukan kerana terlalu malas
dihempap khatulistiwa
panas
terlalu panas
tutuplah matamu
laut masih masin
saya terlupa

kenalkan saya binatang kecil
yang berenang dan merangkak dan menyanyi di paya
menggosok-gosok kaki kecilnya
bagai selama-lamanya
lama-selamanya
saya kan tunggu
retak
pukul
ribut
petir
goncangkan saya
tumbuhkan saya

Loceng berbunyi

Maps, or X Marks the Spot

There is a lot of air in the room.
The weight of the world is beneath your shoes.

Blood-red trucks are good for being seen in on ice-bound islands.

Fogo is the largest of the islands off Newfoundland and Labrador,
Canada. It is northwest of Musgrave Harbour, across Hamilton Sound,
east of Change, 49.6667° North and 54.1833° West.

Fogo is thirty hours away from where I started.

The sea freezes around Fogo.

      I'm fine with not the truth
      This is what I think of
      at the Crossroads of the World
      Past Notre Dame Bay
      A ferry from Farewell

          Hamilton Sound Islands
          North Dog Bay Island
          Handy Harbour
          Woody Island
          Indian Lookout
          Change

                                        Fo
                                        Go

Hearts break   Is
                                        Land
                        every

                                        Tilting

where

Strike a cold fork song into a blue sky day

Fling a tune into the sea

Sing

from your feet on Fogo

The clouds above keep us safe

I have more freedom than I choose

Flight AC861 from London Heathrow (LHR) to Halifax International (YHZ) on Monday, March 25th 2013 took 16h20 and landed at 14.50 local time.

At Halifax airport I spent eight hours:

1. Weighing up the pros and cons of purchasing extremely sugary Canadian snacks
2. Unable to find live lobsters to look at. Ya buy them, take them home and cook 'em. #airports
3. Eating at McDonald's after the sniffer dog found ham sandwiches in my luggage, and
4. Tweeting

At 23.00, I departed for Gander (YQX) and landed at 0.55.
At Gander airport, once called the Crossroads of the World, I lay for five hours staring at:

1. Stationary ceiling fans
2. Woodchip walls
3. The flashing lights of a children's ride bouncing off scratched glass

I also slept.

I dreamt of nothing in particular

I had no nightmares

I rode in a taxi at 5am through flurries of snow

I waited in a room at Farewell

I looked out for seals from an old ferry breaking through ice

I arrived at one of the four corners of the earth and looked
out to sea

Everyone on land had a blood-red truck

I am always at the wrong parties, Duncan Cameron once
said, on a fast train to

Paris

I am always heartbroken, Jonathan Swain said of me, on
the banks of the Thames

On frozen Fire Island

We're off the swivelling compass

Far from the bus stop at the end of the
street

Far from the mango tree

Nothing's up

Everything's out

I'm on the move again

New friends are always beautiful

Hobo stands for 'homeward bound'

The sea freezes around Fogo

A bell rings

Epilogue

Look at where you are. Be there.

1. *This* is one of those tiny, pink, deep-sea prawns that live by underwater volcanoes. They skirt around the mouth of the volcano, where the sea boils and lava jets out from the centre of the earth. They are very small and they live with millions of other prawns, feeding off the carcasses of animals which rain down towards the seabed. These poor creatures die from being poisoned by the noxious deep-sea chemicals. Either that or they have been accidentally swept into the stream and boiled alive. Killed on an underwater flight.

This tiny pink prawn, never having seen sunlight, can only live here.

A bell rings
This sheet falls to the ground

2. This is (Say whatever you'd like. If there are no words, silently count to ten.)

A bell rings
This sheet falls to the ground

3. Now close your eyes.

This is your favourite song washing you clean

your favourite smell

the perfect temperature

the right amount of light on your closed lids

the perfect embrace

Over the music, you hear the people you love most

telling you everything you've ever needed to hear from them

They say everything they've ever needed to say to you

This is—

A bell rings
This sheet falls to the ground

Dark Matter, or This Could Be Anything If Only You'd Sit

I sit

Acknowledgements

Irish Chris (Noel Christopher Giff). Clive Birnie of Burning Eye Books and Bridget Hart for their incredible patience and support over the years. Harriet Evans. Tim Wells. Gloria Sanders, Charles Adrian, Serena Braida who I write for and, when I'm lucky, with. Penny Dimand, Gary Merry, and Jonathan Swain of The New Factory of the Eccentric Actor. David Duchin! Michael Caines without whom there would not have been a Brautigan Book Club. Warren Dent of the Bethnal Green Working Men's Club. Tilly Brooke. Paula Varjack and Dan Simpson who encouraged my chaos. Salena Godden, Bernadette Russell, and Anna Sulan Masing for your flaming hearts, burning generosity and brilliant work. Nikesh Shukla, Chris McCabe, Tessa McWatt, Tim Atkins, Sarah Revivis-Smith, Tina Sederholm, Lara Pawson, Marie McCarthy, Vik Sivalingam, Harold Raitt, KS Chok, and my Bee, Dominic Murphy.

Vera Chok (they/she) is a queer Malaysian-Chinese actor, funny-person, poet and dogmum. They are both Disruptor and Homemaker. Best known as a co-author of *The Good Immigrant*, Vera wrote the chapter, *Yellow*, which exploded ideas around "East Asianness". Vera has been published by The Guardian, Bloomsbury, and Brain Mill Press, and in Rising and Transect magazine. They have been commissioned by The Roundhouse, CNN, WeTransfer, and Hakkasan Group, and funded by The British Council. Their writing has been performed at The Roundhouse, Shakespeare North, Rich Mix, and at Byline, Stoke Newington, Dinefwr, Cambridge, and Bare Lit Festivals. Vera is also a regular participant and sometimes champion of Varjack & Simpson's Anti-Slam. Vera co-founded The Brautigan Book Club, and was a resident artist at the Bethnal Green Working Men's Club. They produce both gently joyful happenings and mischievous, chaotic celebrations to platform historically marginalised groups.

9 781913 958473